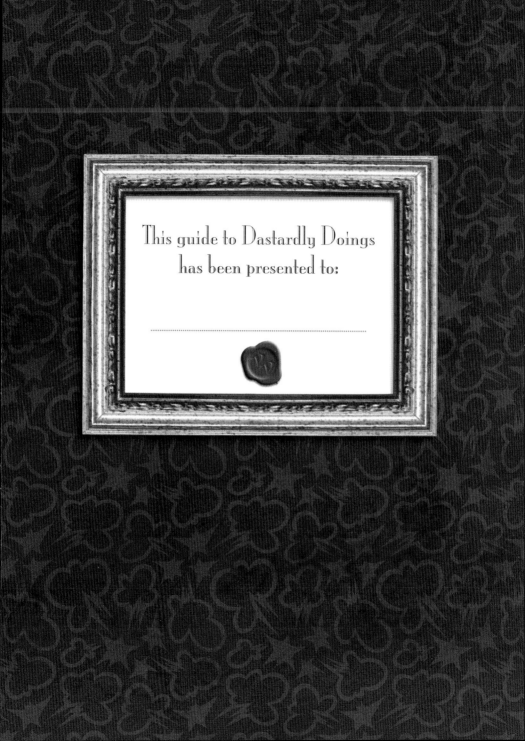

This guide to Dastardly Doings
has been presented to:

....

EGMONT

We bring stories to life

First published 2009 by Egmont UK Limited
239 Kensington High Street, London W8 6SA

Text by Carolyn Madden. Design by Cali Hughes.

ISBN 978 1 4052 4858 7

1 3 5 7 9 10 8 6 4 2

Printed in Singapore

Please note: this book contains risqué humour. It is ideal
for the young at heart, but not suitable for children.

How to Be Dastardly

By Dick Dastardly

EGMONT

Contents

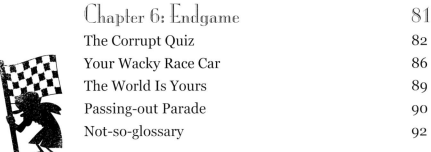

Chapter 1

The World of Arch Villainy

So, you want to be Dastardly, eh?

Well, it doesn't surprise me. History's most infamous figures are often widely emulated. However, I think a little learning is in order: I don't want thousands of carbon copies of myself running around doing the job poorly. If you want to be bad, come with me, friend, and I'll show you our proud history, guide you with tips and top techniques for causing mayhem. From pigeon-catching to winning races in outlandish style, I have a host of cunning tricks up my sleeve, and quite a few more elsewhere. Let me show you a world of badness with the worst do-badding baddies Hanna-Barbera has ever seen.

Kneel before your master.
And ...do something!

The Dick

An interview with Colm N. Tater, pundit on Wacky Races.

66 I race to live and **live to race. 99**

Dastardly
Interview

CT: Welcome, Richard Milhous Dastardly, and thank you for giving us this opportunity to get to know you better.

DD: Yes, yes, get on with it, you dunderhead. I've got things to do and wacky races to win.

CT: Ah, er, quite so. First question . . . Who or what do you most admire?

DD: Myself, of course, you blithering blunderbrain. I am the Reckless Racer, the King of the Road, the epitome of Man and Machine (and Mutt) in perfect harmony! And I'm devilishly handsome too, with fantastic fashion sense. What's not to admire?

CT: Do you believe in the afterlife?

> **❝In my tender youth, I was a trapeze artist, flying through the air with the greatest of ease.❞**

DD: Life after what? I race to live and live to race. Plus, with my track record, I'd rather not think about what's over the finish line, if you see what I mean.

CT: Yes, I do. What's your idea of happiness?

DD: I'd have to say winning. One day – ONE DAY – I will beat those dumb-witted numbskulls, by fair means or foul, and the title will be mine – all MINE! 'Richard M. Dastardly: The World's Wackiest Racer!' *(Drifts off into a reverie . . .)*

CT: Ahem! Back to the interview: what's the worst job you've had?

DD: In my tender youth, I was a trapeze artist, flying through the air with the greatest of ease, until one day a painful accident proved my downfall and, since then, *(stifled sob)* my moustache has curled slightly at the ends.

But the worst ever is that curs'd Flying Ace job. It may look glamorous: the aeroplanes, the weaponry, the henchmen; but talk about lack of job satisfaction!

Those cartooning buffoons at Hanna-Barbera never let me catch that feathered fool. If only I could get close enough, just once, then Birdy would be mincemeat and the medals would be mine!

CT: What's your perfect car?

DD: The *Mean Machine*, of course! It has every design feature and booby trap a fiend could dream of, from can-openers to catapults, and magnets to moustache wax! And it's a dastardly shade of purple.

CT: What's your favourite cocktail?

DD: A Molotov. There's nothing so refreshing as a small explosion, mid-race.

CT: Why are the baddies more interesting than the goodies?

DD: The definitions 'baddie' and 'goodie' are rather subjective, don't you think? We're all in the race to win it. I ask you, if I use my vastly superior intelligence to foil the others, is that

❝ There's nothing so refreshing as a small explosion, mid-race. ❞

so very wrong? However, there is something of the 'dashing cad' about my look. Against that puffed-up pepper pot Peter Perfect, I may exude a certain roguish charm . . . *(Twirls moustache, suavely.)*

CT: Is Muttley as dumb as he looks?

DD: Muttley? Dumb? He could have

❝ It may look glamorous: the aeroplanes, the weaponry, the henchmen; but talk about lack of job satisfaction! ❞

written the book on 'Dumb' – except that he *can't* write. That chortling chump couldn't catch a cold without my help! No, I am the brains behind the operation, and if we haven't won a race or caught a pigeon yet, it's down to that mutt's misguided meddling . . . *(wanders off, muttering darkly.)*

THE GREAT SATURDAY

> Braced to race are Saturday morning's cartoon champs, or should that be chumps? Stop sniggering, Muttley, and let's see who's at the starting grid . . . oh and er, pass those tacks, will you?

COLM N. TATER'S BOOTH

1: YOGI BEAR

First in the line-up is that bone-headed bear, Yogi. "Smarter than the average bear", eh? There's nothing but jelly(stone) under his porkpie hat *(cackles at own joke)*. And what about Boo Boo? Hardly going to send Ranger Smith running to hide in a pic-a-nic basket, is he?

MORNING RACE

2: THE FLINTSTONES

Second on the starting grid is Fred Flintstone. The cretinous caveman won't get far in that pile of rubble . . . and talking of which, there's that bozo Barney too, one genetic step up from lichen. It'll take more than pebble-power to beat me! From Bedrock's bottom to the most tip-top, it's . . .

3: TOP CAT

Bah, next up is the King of Cons, Top Cat and his mangy moggies. Look at those facile felines, they can't even outwit that twit, Dibble. They'll never cat-ch me!

4: THE JETSONS

The only serious competition in this race is the Jetsons: their jetcar can travel at over 5,500 mph. But that George Jetson's a goof and no match for the cunning of yours truly. Those Jetsons won't see me for space dust. *(Chortle.)*

5: TOUCHÉ TURTLE

Why, if it isn't that swashbuckling shellback, Touché Turtle, and his aptly named sidekick, Dum Dum! No little green reptile is going to hammer me! Touché away . . . back to your pond, Beaky.

6: SECRET SQUIRREL

Next on the grid is that bouffant-bottomed rodent, Secret Squirrel, and his bespectacled buddy, Morocco Mole. What's so secret about a bushy buffoon in a holey hat, I'd like to know. He's barely a match for that cravat-wearing chump, Yellow Pinkie, let alone the Moustached Marvel! *(That's me, you fool.)*

7: HONG KONG PHOOEY

That number one super guy, Hong Kong Phooey, can transform the Phooeymobile into any vehicle at the bong of the gong. Well, let him try to chop his way to the top – he's got Dick Dastardly to beat first. The troublesome Spot may be more of a problem . . . Pussycat, Muttley! Chase him, you canine clown!

8: DICK DASTARDLY & MUTTLEY

And last up – but only until the race begins – it's me! The other Wacky drivers may cheat their way to glory, but surely I'll win against this trackful of turkeys. Muttley, stop sniggering and *do something*!

My Big Book of Naughtiness

by Dick Dastardly

Welcome to my private library, an inspirational place where I dream and scheme, studying my Big Book of Naughtiness and avoiding the demonic, yellow glare of my half-crazed muses.

Here's what you've all been waiting for: the real baddies! Even I, the most malevolent of miscreants, bow down (gibbering and cringing slightly) before such glorious foulness. Weep with fear as you meet Saturday morning's WORST villains.

Ah, who's this handsome fellow . . . ?

NAME: Richard Milhous Dastardly

AKA: Dick Dastardly, Rick Rastardly (Muttley)

DESCRIPTION: debonair flying ace, with goggles and dashing purple coat

NEMESES : Wacky Racers, Yankee Doodle Pigeon

MOTIVATION: to win the glorious title of 'The World's Wackiest Racer' and to stop that pigeon – NOW!

METHOD OF MENACE: a catalogue of booby traps and devices – all extremely cunning and not at all likely to backfire

HENCHMAN: Muttley, a dog

SPECIAL SKILLS: a genius of extreme cunning and charm

DD RATING: 10/10. What can I say? I have it all. Read about me and weep, bad guys!

23

NAME: The Hooded Claw

AKA: Sylvester Sneekly (Clawy to his friends . . . well, he might be if he had any friends)

DESCRIPTION: green cape, sneaky purple eye-mask, you can't miss him

NEMESIS: Penelope Pitstop

MOTIVATION: heir to Penelope's fortune

METHOD OF MENACE: elaborate plots to kill Penelope. Plots include dropping her from a plane into a box of wildcats and pea-shooting her horse

HENCHMEN: the Bully Brothers, two bully brothers

SPECIAL SKILLS: has a penchant for shooting pretty women from cannons; excellent line in put-downs

DD RATING: 3/10. Looks good but tends to tie up Penelope and leave her somewhere . . . so she usually escapes

NAME: Yellow Pinkie

AKA: Oi, Baldy! (There are no surviving users of this nickname)

DESCRIPTION: a cravat-sporting baldy (but don't tell him I said so)

NEMESIS: Secret Squirrel

MOTIVATION: world domination

METHOD OF MENACE: specialises in lasers (rather clichéd, if you ask me)

HENCHMAN: the Cravat (cameo appearance)

SPECIAL SKILLS: disarmingly charming, usually warns victim of the method of their demise; allergic to rodents

DD RATING: 7/10. I rather feel his name lets him down

25

NAME: Black Knight

AKA: Creaky Pants (to his mum)

DESCRIPTION: a black knight

NEMESIS:
Touché Turtle

MOTIVATION:
fair maidens

**METHOD OF
MENACE:**
abduction

HENCHMAN: works alone

SPECIAL SKILLS: has an eye
for the ladies; great with his lance;
bit moody

DD RATING: 9/10. The Dastardlys
admire fellows who have a way with
the ladies, as we do. Plus (ahem), he
makes me nervous

NAME: Dr Zin

AKA: nothing you'd live to repeat

DESCRIPTION: fiendish skull head with yellow skin and diabolical laugh

NEMESIS: Jonny Quest

MOTIVATION: money and power by any means

METHOD OF MENACE: two-way TV screen to reveal his hand in a plot; uses henchmen (such as a giant robot spider) for dirty work

HENCHMEN: a selection of horrors including a giant robotic spider

SPECIAL SKILLS: puts the 'ill' into 'villain' . . . he appears to be ailing but keeps popping up behind dastardly plots

DD RATING: 6/10. I admire his persistence, but he really should get some sun

NAME: Gemini

AKA: Two-Face

DESCRIPTION: evil wizard with spooky spinning head with two faces: the 'kindly aged uncle' face and the 'bloodied eye sockets' one

NEMESIS: Thundarr the Barbarian

MOTIVATION: oh, the usual... to become 'Supreme Ruler', 'Master of the Most Powerful Magic', and so on

METHOD OF MENACE: sorcery and sinister behaviour

HENCHMAN: the Groundling, a strange rat-like man, or man-like rat... not pretty either way

SPECIAL SKILLS: he's got eyes in the back of his head. No, really...

DD RATING: 8/10. High score for his weird 'little old man' voice

NAME: The Council of Doom

(Pronounced "Thar Cown-sil awf Do-OOO-OOO-mmm")

AKA: Zorak (insectoid alien), Brak (catoid alien), Metallus (robot), Moltar, Creature King, Spider Woman (aka the Black Widow)

DESCRIPTION: lots of really bad baddies who've teamed up against Space Ghost

NEMESIS: Space Ghost

MOTIVATION: to get that pesky Space Ghost and tie a knot in him

METHOD OF MENACE: you name it, they've tried it all

HENCHMEN: a selection of nasties

SPECIAL SKILLS: don't turn your back on this lot

DD RATING: 3/10. They may look the part, but six against one and they still haven't stopped that caped chump, Space Ghost

ARCH-VILLAIN KNOCK OUT

So, you've met the bad guys. Now it's time to throw them into the ring together to see who'd come out Chump, er, Champ . . . My money would be on me, but it's no contest so I'll play referee. Whaddaya mean? It's my book!

ARCH-VILLAIN KNOCK OUT
ROUND I
CLAW vs PINKIE

The Hooded Claw.

First up is the Hooded Claw vs Yellow Pinkie. 'DING! DING!' There's the bell! The Hooded Claw swoops in there with the über-baddie name, but Pinkie's jab-jab-jabbing with his high-tech laser weapons. The Hooded Claw takes another thrashing thanks to his ostentatious outfit . . . whereas you might ask the smartly attired Pinkie for the time before he zapped you to death. Claw's on his knees but takes a jab at Baldy, er, Pinkie, for having a

Yellow 'Baldy' Pinkie.

squirrel for an enemy. But Pinkie's in there with the knock-out punch: Claw's enemy wears lipstick. Yellow Pinkie wins the bout!

YELLOW PINKIE WINS THE BOUT!

ARCH-VILLAIN KNOCK OUT
ROUND II
BLACK KNIGHT VS DR ZIN

Black Knight.

The well-polished, Dr Zin.

Next, we take a walk on the dark side. In the red corner, weighing in at a few more pounds than the fair maidens would like, it's the gallant talent . . . Black Knight! His opponent today has magic in his gloves and fire in his heart.

That's right, ladies and gentlemen, in the blue corner we have the talismanic, the enigmatic, the wizard with the chin . . . it's Dr Zin! 'DING! DING!' The bell rings, and the fight gets underway! Knighty's in there first with a body blow, thanks to his devilish name; Dr Zin sounds like a cleaning product. But Zin's off the ropes and leading in the looks stakes, with his shiny skull head versus Black Knight's rather camp suit of armour. But what's this? Knighty gets out his lance and it's all over – Black Knight is disqualified for inappropriate use of his weapon. Muttley, stop sniggering, you floppy-eared hound!

DR ZIN WINS!

ARCH-VILLAIN KNOCK OUT
ROUND III
GEMINI vs COUNCIL OF DOOM

Gemini left the iron on ...

The Council of Domesticity.

We're in for a barnburner of a fight tonight. It is sure to be an epic! Wearing the red shorts is a journeyman from the post-apocalyptic wasteland we call 'the future'; a brawler with eyes in the back of his ugly head . . . Oh my, it's the evil wizard, Gemini! His opponents are a collection of misfits whose last bout was with the punch-drunk Space Ghost. In the blue corner, wearing matching blue shorts, I give you the Cown-sil awf Do-OOO-OOO-mmm! Hang on, what's this? Gemini's weird henchman, the rat-like Groundling, is jumping up and down. There's been a late announcement from The Council of Doom: they've had to go home because they left the iron on. Gemini looks worried. Where is he going? Come back, you can't all have left the iron on! Talk about glass-jawed clowns . . . it's a no contest, Muttley!

RESULT VOID — FIGHT ABANDONED.

THE FINAL BOUT

And now to the fight we've all been waiting for: still left in the competition are Yellow Pinkie and Dr Zin. Who will be crowned über-baddie?

YELLOW PINKIE vs DR ZIN

Baldy loser!

As the two fighters touch gloves, the tension builds. Pinkie straightens his cravat – nerves, perhaps? Is he concealing illegal laser weapons down his shorts? Dr Zin is motionless, is he dead? No! He raises his hands, he adopts the Piano pose, and Pinkie crumples to the ground. Drat, drat and double drat! It's all over before the bell has even rung, Dr Zin has

The champion, Dr Zin.

used the dirtiest of all dirty tricks – magic.

DR ZIN IS CHAMPION OF THE RING.

Apart from me.

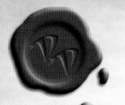

Fiendishness

The Dastardlys have wormed their way through the pages of History – each blackguard more criminally minded than the next. So, you see, it's genetic. Come, meet the family.

Dickus Dastardicus

Crime committed 142 AD

My Roman forebear was an important man, chief engineer in charge of building the Antonine Wall in Scotland, no less. A rapscallion of the highest order, Dickus charged the Emperor Antoninus Pius for building a stone wall but, in fact, got his cronies to make one from turf and pocketed the profits, (chortle). No one knows what happened to him – but there is a village called Dastardaievka in Siberia . . .

Through the Ages

Dickfred of Dastard

Crime committed 871AD

Dickfred was my Anglo-Saxon ancestor. He was an envoy to King Alfred the Great, but the sneaky scoundrel slipped some maps and whatnot to the Vikings. At last, his duplicity – how sweet the word – was rumbled, and Dickfred ended up in the stocks. Anyone for (rotten) cabbage?

Richard the Dastardly

Crime committed 1328AD

As a nobleman at the court of Edward III, but in the pay of the Scots, Richard persuaded the king to cede victory to Robert the Bruce. Then the cheeky knave popped in on Brucey and asked him for a lairdship, no less. He was last seen doggy-paddling across Loch Lomond, sporting a strange (swim)suit of tar and feathers.

Ricardo Dastardos

Crime committed 1588AD

It would seem, dear reader, that my noble genes made it back to mainland Europe, where Ricardo was a captain in the Spanish Armada. According to eyewitnesses, when Ricardo's ship came in sight of the English fleet, it appeared to waver and then vanished into the mist. Superstitious English sailors believed Ricardo to be sailing a ghost ship; the Spanish knew better. Alas, we Dastardlys will never know what became of our Spanish cousin.

Ricky Dastard

Crime committed 1753AD

Ricky was also a captain, this time of a less-than-glamorous coal boat that sailed between Newcastle and London. This miscreant was caught trying to sell the Geordies their own coals and was promptly transported to America. At this proud moment in time, our ancestral colonisation of America began.

Ritchie Dastardly

Crime committed 1839AD

According to criminal records,
Ritchie was a petty fraudster in
California, but perhaps too, he
was a diviner. In 1839, he forged
documents declaring that gold
had been found on his scrubby
Sacramento Valley farm, and flogged
the worthless land to John Sutter,
a Swiss settler, for $400. So far, so
good. However, in January 1848 gold
was discovered on that farm, and it
triggered the start of the gold rush.
Legend has it that, on moonlit nights
in the Sutter's Mill area, you can
still hear Ritchie's ghost howling:
"Drat, drat and double drat!"

Dick 'the Goon' Dastardly

Crime committed 14 February 1929AD

The Goon was part of Al Capone's
gang (clearly Capone had an eye
for talent). On St Valentine's Day,
he was posted as lookout during an
operation to ambush Bugs Moran.
Mistaking one of Bugs Moran's
gang for the boss, Bugs himself, the
Goon gave the signal that Bugs was
approaching and Capone's gang
opened fire. Arriving late, the target,
Bugs, doubled-back when he heard
shooting and nipped off for a coffee.
That night, the Goon was said to be
sleeping with the fishes, whatever
that means; we may be scoundrels,
but we're not weirdos.

Chapter 2

How to Be Dastardly

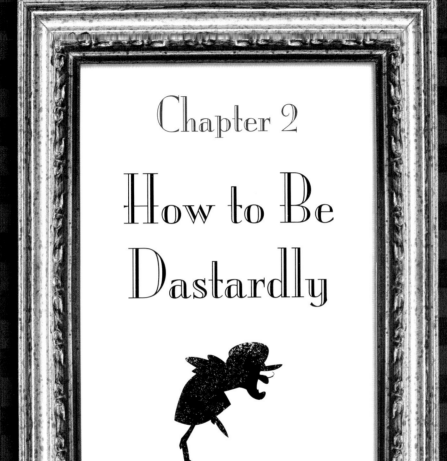

Get the Dastardly Look

An improbably large hat not only gives you those all-important inches where it matters, enabling 'Towering Above Victims' to be executed effectively, it also provides a handy store for minor explosives, rodents or, indeed, your picnic when on the road.

Goggles lend the wearer an air of nonchalance, no matter if you can't see through them. Wear them upside down, Dastardly style, for added devil-may-care attitude.

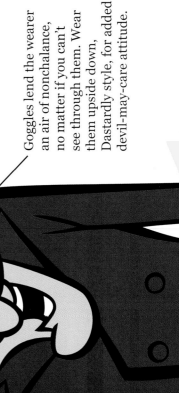

For the Arch Villain, image is God. So, if you want to be bad, you've got to dress bad. Stop sniggering, Muttley! First impressions count: how would you anticipate my fiendish cunning if I weren't the Prince of Purple? Follow my tips to cut a dash.

A waxed 'tache tells 'em you're a winner. Curl the ends for a look that's pure mischievous rogue.

No villain would be properly attired without the appropriate undergarments for warmth and support. The Dastardlys have used the same fabric for generations. I'll say no more.

Dashing leather flying gloves, styled after genuine US Military Issue circa 1914.

Nothing says, "I'm a maverick" like a frock coat. Choose a colour to complement your vehicle of choice. Purple is regal yet hints at a dark side. Camouflage could prove problematic as it tends to draw sniper fire.

41

A Schemer's Guide

Bye, bye, Penelope!

So, my dear reader, the admirable fiend Dick Dastardly has left you in my company to talk Villainy. As someone who cultivates anti-social tendencies, I will enjoy guiding you through some of the malevolent motives that lurk behind my evil schemes.

to Villainous Motives

No.1: Inheritance

We all like something for nothing, and this is the ultimate in easy gains! All you need to do is suck up to a wealthy relative over a period of several years. This may involve having to listen endlessly to stories entitled 'In My Day', while eating cake with a sell-by date of 1913. But, remember, the best things come to those who wait. Take the time to convince them of your worthiness. Pay particular regard to those orphans you're sponsoring. Pick up shopping for them. I suggest you take a little commission on top to keep you focused.

If all this sounds too taxing, try the short, sharp method: find a rich person and bump off their heir, ensuring that you're next in line beforehand. It could be that the shock of losing a loved one will shuffle them along a bit too.

Hanging out with Miss Pitstop!

The Belle's fortune shall be mine!

No. 2: Treasure

Now, we all need to spoil ourselves from time to time so get out there and purloin someone else's ill-gotten gains. If the goods are illicit, they can't very well call in the law, can they? Beware of trying this with the Ant Hill Mob, or you may find yourself waking up with Seabiscuit in your bed.

Pirates are easy targets: look for anyone with one leg and a parrot, saying, "Ah-har me hearties!" Slip them a few rums in the pub, then follow them late at night. They may lead you to their pieces of eight . . . or to fast food. Either way, you win.

No. 3: Power

Power is the bridge between wealth and world domination. And it's addictive. If you've got what it takes to be an Arch Villain, wealth will never be enough. Once you've made yourself as rich as Cresus, you'll be so brimming with self-regard, you may feel the urge to share what you have with others . . . but only on your terms. That's what *real* power is.

No. 4: World Domination

This one is only for the major players, so if you're having trouble lying about your sugar intake, you're not in this league yet. Practise stealing candy from a baby instead. However, if misdeeds are your forte and you have access to a space station, subterranean nuclear power station or sub-aquatic city, read on . . . It's really very simple. Take what other people have then threaten to destroy it unless they give you land/money/a space station. Eventually you will become a superpower in your own right . . . The most villainous the world has ever seen!

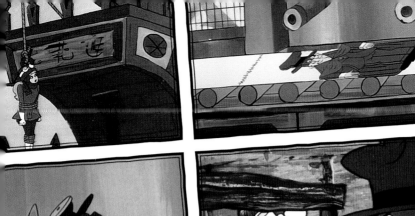

Self-help for Super-villains

You've got the look, you've schemed some schemes, but here, dear reader, your fiend – er, friend – Dick Dastardly will nurture your villainous mindset. So, what are you waiting for? Stop snivelling and read on! By the way, I was trying to spot a prompt or mnemonic of some kind to help you remember my pearls of wisdom, but none emerged.

Image

A sneaky snigger is essential, as is a fiendish grin; the goggles are not. Practise your grimace in the mirror daily and in any reflective window you pass (apart from school windows).

Make sure you sneak away from the scene of wrongdoing with your hands raised to chest height, fingers poised in 'piano' position.

Remember, be seen with a sidekick, if only to have someone to blame for the funny smell. The best henchmen are interchangeable. If they have identities of their own, they're probably not stupid enough – and you can't risk them literally stealing the show.

Disguise

Don't worry about your disguise, dear reader: the worse it is, the less likely it is that people will see through it. Penelope Pitstop still hasn't spotted that the Hooded Claw is her Uncle.

He is? Oh, he-y-lp! HE-Y-LP!

Just because you are a super-villain, doesn't mean you have to shroud yourself in black. Indeed, this can be a bit of a giveaway. Ring the changes with Icky-goo Green or Lanced Boil Purple for your cloak and mask. No one will expect a thing, allowing you to go unnoticed about your dastardly deeds.

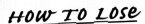

HOW TO LOSE

There's no such thing as a good loser, losing sucks. So when the chips are down – on the fuzzy carpet – don't just stand there and accept it with good grace. What is the use of bottling up all that frustration? No, you need to shout, stamp and scream like a sugar-saturated schoolchild. If your slogan doesn't really work, try: "Drat, drat and double drat!" Embrace the shame.

> Drat, drat and double DRAT!

Indestructibility*

Remember, if you get hurt, you won't feel it because you're only a cartoon. This is a useful tip when a plan turns out not to be completely foolproof, after all, and you are sawn in half by a runaway circular saw. Just pick yourself up (both halves), dust yourself down and start all over again.

Heavy objects (anvils, boulders, etc.) coming into contact with your skull result in stars circling your head and comic sound effects, rather than anything more severe.

Objective

Decide what your goal is and stick to it. I've managed to keep chasing after prizes and pigeons since 1968, and it hasn't done me any harm.

"Stay focused, stay mean, don't become a has-been!" (I say, that's rather good!) could have been my mantra, if I didn't already have the splendid, "Drat, drat and double drat!"

Talk the Talk

Reader, get yourself a slogan now – the more improbable, the better. "I'll get you, Penelope Pitstop!" is a classic example. The more often you fail to act on your threats, the more absurd you look, but you'll find ranting will keep your spirits up. See The Catchphrase Generator (page 51) if you really are too stupid to come up with your own.

* These survival tips should only be attempted by 2-D fictional characters. No liability for injury or death sustained as a result of these tips shall be undertaken by the publisher, licensor or any member of the *Wacky Races* team.

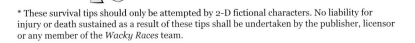

How Not to Be Bad...

*To underline the skill it takes to be that superior being, the Arch Villain, permit me to show you how it should **not** be done. Presenting these poor specimens can only serve to heighten the glory of the Knights of Naughtiness (my favourite after-dinner joke).*

Officer Dibble

Here we have a poor, pathetic morsel, an officer of the law, no less, who is frequently wrong-footed by a cat. Yes, a cat! The dithering Dibble tries to oust Top Cat and the gang from the alley on Dibble's patch where TC masterminds scams, without success. Only when TC's elaborate schemes backfire, does Dibble get one over on him. And it's my belief that he's got a soft spot for that puddy tat. The great dope.

Of course, one must maintain standards; I only apply the name 'baddie' to Dibble because he's the antagonist to that persuasive puss, the creature who truly deserves the title 'anti-hero', Top Cat. It reminds me of something TC himself once said: "I've been using my brains for years. Officer Dibble's is practically brand new."

Ranger Smith

Look at this specimen. This withering excuse for a warden is repeatedly outwitted by a greedy teddy bear. See the weak chin, the beetling brows? Signs of a lesser being. A baddie that's only bad enough to bully bears. What is Cartoonville coming to?

Mr Jinks

Now for our next pathetic example, Mr Jinks. A creature to whom the term 'bad' refuses to stick, less it be sullied by association. This shambolic example of feline wiles is repeatedly thwarted in his attempts to rid his house of mice. He may 'hate those meeces to pieces' but he's hopelessly incompetent at resolving the issue. Think rat poison, Kitty.

Conclusion

These are but a few of the many poor examples of badness, I will not dignify them with the name 'villain'. Reader, I see a question forming in your mind, a glimmer of rebellion in that puddle of dark jelly, you're thinking that I am a poor example of badness too. Reader . . . friend . . . how could you? I plan my moves with Machiavellian accuracy and practise my art with great skill – yet still that pigeon escapes me! Arrggh!

I'm smarter than the average bear!

TOUCHÉ AWAY!

Rassuh-frazza-pazza . . .

Jane, stop this crazy thing.

Drat, drat and DOUBLE DRAT!

I'll get you, Penelope Pitstop! HYU-HYU-HYU-HUH-HUH-HUH . . . etc.

Muttleyyyy! DO something!

Heheheheee!

Muttley, you snickering, floppy-eared hound. When courage is needed, you're never around. Those medals you wear on your moth-eaten chest should be there for bungling at which you are best!

Rassum brassum mshlsssl Rick Rastardly!

You've seen some of the finest catchphrases the world of Hanna-Barbera has to offer. Now it's time to create your own. Even the biggest chumps should be able to create a dastardly phrase with my Catchphrase Generator – yes, just play around with the words, Einstein!

A.C.M.E. CATCHPHRASE GENERATOR

HE'LL	NEVER GET	MINCEMEAT	ME
I'LL	GET	IT	TURKEY
YOU'LL	BE	HA	WITH IT
DON'T THINK YOU'LL	HA	AWAY	FOOL
HA	REGRET	MEDDLING	HA

How to Spot the Goodies

'The Goodie'. Come, friend, let us look at this strange specimen and pinpoint its key features. Then we can ensure that we don't blunder when trying to undermine their good intentions. Now follow me . . .

Peter Perfect

This musclebrain puts the 'jock' into strap. A pompous puppet, designed to make my hackles rise, with his shiny skin and skintight pants. *Turbo Terrific*! Of all the ridiculous names for a car . . . especially one that falls apart whenever the door slams! (Must calm down, my dear Dickie, it's bad for the old ticker.)

Key features: sickeningly clean-cut and athletic. Bah! Silly clothes, silly smile, silly dolt! He's asking to be tricked.

Methodology: he's prone to preening — hand him a mirror and you can just take whatever you want.

Penelope Pitstop

Don't be fooled by this pretty pink lady. Beneath the smog of perfume and lacquer, there's a gal that really knows what she wants and how to get it. Peter Perfect (grrrr) has his eye on her and, bizarrely, she seems to return his affections. She must think that I'm out of her league.

Key features: pretty, pink and perfect. Knows how to use her wiles.

Methodology: dupe with extreme caution.

Jonny Quest

I ask you, reader, it comes to something when the Goodies put up a child. Is that their trump card? Master Quest is blond, keen and squeaky clean. Talk about taking candy from a baby . . . problem is, unless you want a truth serum or an Egyptian deity statue, there's not much candy to take.

Key features: small, annoying.

Methodology: swindle if you can be bothered but watch out for his brainy father, mystical friend and muscle-bound bodyguard.

Fred Flintstone

Well, this numbskull shouldn't be hard to cheat, he'll do anything for a flutter or a game. Trouble is there's nothing you'd want to trick him out of . . . unless you covet his pet snorkasaurus.

Key features: doltish grin. Manky fur mini-dress. Steamroller-style automobile.

Methodology: any kind of cheap con will work. Try card tricks . . . this prehistoric pinhead hasn't seen paper yet!

Chapter 3

Henchmen
and
Sidekicks

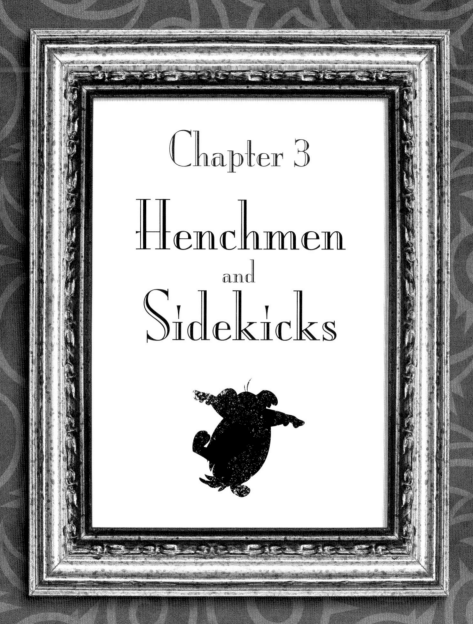

What to Look for in a Stooge

A henchman. A stooge. A sidekick. Call it what you may, a companion is a must-have for any self-respecting baddie. But not just any old sidekick will do; you must seek out certain 'qualities' to enhance your own image.

WHAT?

A sidekick is a right-hand man, a fall guy and a kicking boy. They're there for three important reasons: to help you when you need a second pair of hands; to blame when things go wrong; and most importantly, to make you look good. Heh-heh-heh!

WHY?

Your stooge is there to boost your status, fellow fiend, so ensure that you select a specimen with poor physical presence who ideally lacks any personality. Take Muttley, for example. He's so moth-eaten that even bacteria refuse to colonise him. So why feed him? Why look after him? Because, friend, the miserable mutt lacks any charisma, and his loss is my gain as I appear all the more debonair. Plus he can fly an aeroplane.

HOW?

As we all studied at school, and mine was a particularly mis-er-able learning curve, gang mentality means that your worth is greater than the sum of your parts, meaning, numbskull, that I look bigger and better with Muttley by my side than alone.

WHERE?

Well, at your right hand, you dolt, where else would your right-hand man be?

WHEN?

I'm sick of these stupid questions. He's there all the time. Whenever a race is to be won or a pigeon to be chased – er, caught. Satisfied?

KEY FEATURES:

Strange shaggy coat:
would make anything else look
à la mode, but contrast it with a chic
purple frock coat and you're fodder
fit for the catwalk.

Cheap-and-nasty flying helmet:
a poor imitation of my handcrafted
headgear.

Ridiculously dopey grin:
enhances my strong jaw
and – shall we say –
mis-chee-vous smile.

Overblown pride:
contrasts with
my decorous
demeanour.

Clownish stance:
the dope thinks he's in for a medal
but unless there's one for Extreme
Stupidity, he wrong. Compare, dear
reader, my own proud poise. Breeding
shows. Likewise inbreeding.

Life According

An interview with Colm N. Tater, pundit on Wacky Races.

> **Rat Rik Rastardree snacken fracken bracken groof.**

Greetings, baddie wannabes! I'm Colm N. Tater, your very own pundit on *Wacky Races.* I'm here today to chat with Muttley the mutt.

CT Muttley, thank you for joining us in the interview suite where your boss sat just pages before. So, what motivates you, Muttley?

MUTTLEY Medals. Yeah, yeah, yeah, yeah, yeah. Gimme, gimme, gimme!

CT I see. And what is your take on the (anti)hero, Dick Dastardly?

MUTTLEY Rat Rik Rastardree snacken fracken bracken groof.

CT Er, quite so. Why do you continue to work with him when he treats you so badly?

to Muttley

66 Medals. Yeah, yeah, yeah, yeah. Gimme, gimme, gimme! 99

MUTTLEY Medals. Yeah, yeah, yeah, yeah, yeah. Gimme, gimme, gimme!

CT Do you ever seek revenge?
MUTTLEY Rep. Hee, hee, hee, hee, hee, hee, hee! Muttrey prut brell ron Rastardree's red. Muttrey hrit brell rif hrammer – DRONGGGG! Hee, hee, hee, hee, hee, hee, hee!

CT Er, I see . . . And finally, Muttley, what advice do you have to inspire our wannabe baddies?
MUTTLEY Medals. Yeah, yeah, yeah, yeah. Gimme, gimme, gimme, gimme!

Um, well, wasn't that enlightening? Thank you, Muttley.

(Muttley sniggers.)

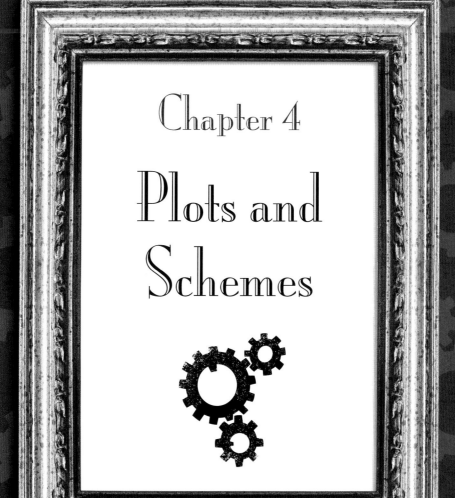

Chapter 4

Plots and Schemes

ANTI YANKEE DOODLE

So, wanna-be-baddie, you must learn to scheme your schemes and plan your manoeuvres with military precision. Herewith are two of my finest schemes. Sadly, neither was successful – but that's thanks to the blithering fools in the Vulture Squadron. Look and learn, my friend, look and learn.

FIG. 2
Target crosses line between planes

FIG. 3
Pitcher throws ball and batter strikes

FIG. 4
Ball opens and swallows target

FLYING FORMATIONS

THE BASEBALL MANOEUVRE

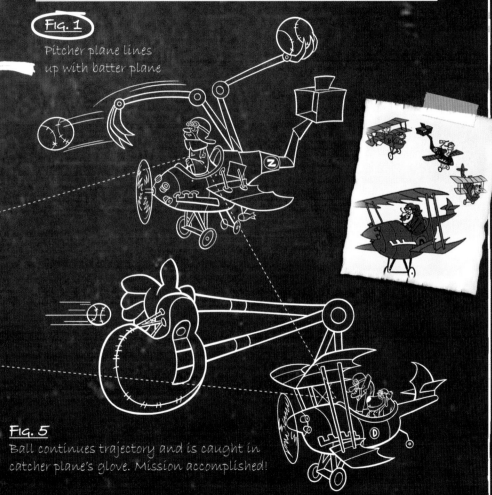

Fig. 1
Pitcher plane lines
up with batter plane

Fig. 5
Ball continues trajectory and is caught in
catcher plane's glove. Mission accomplished!

CUCKOO CLOCK AMBUSH

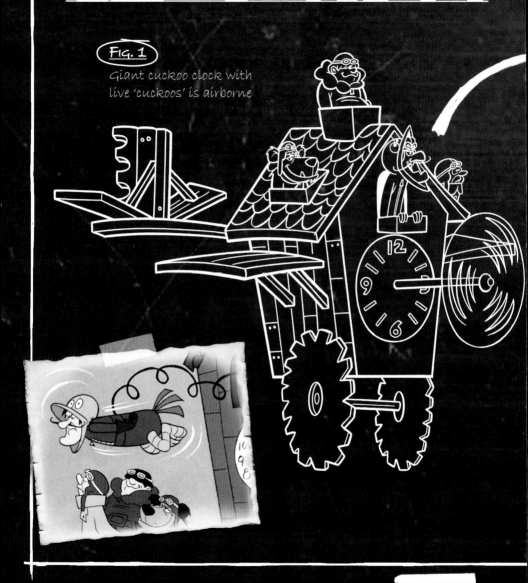

FIG. 1

Giant cuckoo clock with live 'cuckoos' is airborne

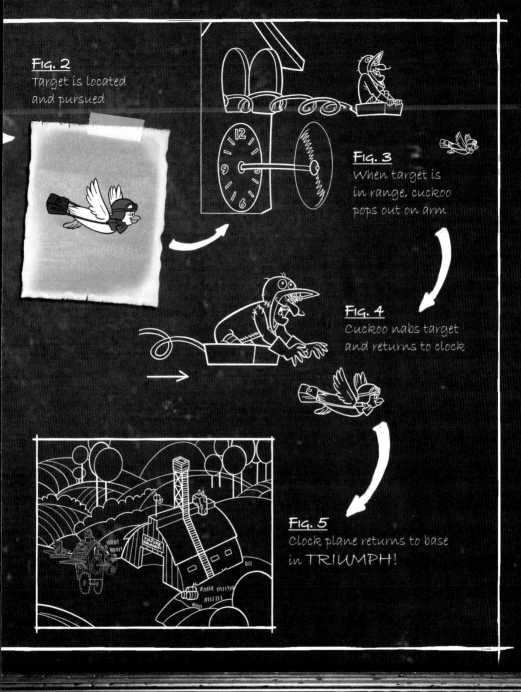

Fig. 2
Target is located and pursued

Fig. 3
When target is in range, cuckoo pops out on arm

Fig. 4
Cuckoo nabs target and returns to clock

Fig. 5
Clock plane returns to base in TRIUMPH!

Top Tips for Dastardly Doings

Herewith, dear friend, foul fiend, whatever . . . I've outlined some malignant plots to inspire you. Look no further than the schemes that my wicked counterparts and I have devised.

Low-down Tricks

Who better to learn from than that Sultan of Self-Interest, the all tip-top Top Cat? Like all good plans, his best scam is simple but effective. When tipping a waiter/doorman, he simply ties the coin with a piece of string, which is whisked straight out of the waiter/doorman's hand and back into his pocket as he walks away. Tip-top tipping tip, Top Cat!

Doctor O

This insidious possum and his Bat Boys devised a plan so cunning that even Secret Squirrel was left in the dark. Among their light-exterminating devices was the satellite with giant hands, which cast Earth into darkness. Being nocturnal, the shady sneakers could operate well in the dark. Unfortunately for him, so could Morocco Mole. But you have to admire his audacity.

The Dirty Dozen:
DOs and DON'Ts for Do-Badders

1. DO look sinister
2. DON'T look down
3. DO wear an unconvincing disguise
4. DON'T work with animals
5. DO sneak
6. DON'T confess
7. DO chuckle evilly
8. DON'T give up
9. DO win the race
10. DON'T forget your bag of dirty tricks
11. DO catch that pigeon – now!
12. DON'T ever play fair

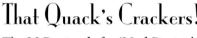

That Quack's Crackers!

The M.D. stands for 'Mad Doctor', so, dear reader, you will not be surprised to learn that it was Dr Crankenshaft who created the Gobbling Glob. This blue glob grew as it ate, eating as it grew, until it was set to conquer the world for the M.D. But Crankenshaft reckoned without that peanut-sized pest, Atom Ant, and world domination was put on hold for another day.

Road Race Tactics

Racing manoeuvres and tactics offer a challenging gauntlet to the wackiest racers. Come with me, fiend, and learn from the Master. I have a huge variety of devices available at the push of a button on my dashboard. Below, I have outlined my preferred methods for, er, shall we say, disadvantaging my fellow racers.

1

CHARACTERS: The Slag Brothers (Rock and Gravel)
VEHICLE: Bouldermobile
METHOD: a large hammer is set off by a tripwire laid over the racetrack, smashing the Bouldermobile to tiny pieces.

2

CHARACTERS: The Gruesome Twosome
VEHICLE: Creepy Coupé
METHOD: a fiendish skull-and-crossbones sign at the side of the road points the dimwitted duo into a dark cave.

3

CHARACTER: Professor Pat Pending
VEHICLE: Convert-a-car
METHOD: a cattle grid embedded into the road traps the Convert-a-car's narrow front bicycle wheel.

4

CHARACTER: Red Max
VEHICLE: Crimson Haybailer
METHOD: a ramp channels the Haybailer off the road and into mid-air. It soars gloriously through the sky before coming to an abrupt stop in a tree top.

5

CHARACTER: Penelope Pitstop
VEHICLE: Compact Pussycat
METHOD: a mirror positioned by the side of the road causes Penelope to stop to check her reflection. The Anthill Mob and Peter Perfect stop to assist her.

6

CHARACTERS: Sergeant Blast and Private Meekly
VEHICLE: Army Surplus Special
METHOD: a blob of chewing gum on the road sticks to the steamroller wheel, causing it to stick around!

7

CHARACTERS: The Ant Hill Mob
VEHICLE: Bullet-proof Bomb
METHOD: see No 5. What is it about that Southern gal? The flowing blonde hair? The sweet-smelling perfume? She's nothing compared to my dear Dolores.

8

CHARACTERS: Lazy Luke and Blubber Bear
VEHICLE: Chuggabug
METHOD: a giant waterbomb dropped by Muttley from a cliff extinguishes the Chuggabug's coal-fired engine.

9

CHARACTER: Peter Perfect
VEHICLE: Turbo Terrific (a terrible name for a car!)
METHOD: see No 5. With his silly clothes, silly hair, silly muscles - Peter Perfect is just asking to be tricked!

10

CHARACTERS: Rufus Ruffcut and Sawtooth
VEHICLE: The Buzzwagon
METHOD: lumberjack Rufus drives over a nest of termites, which eat the wooden wagon. The irony so pleases me.

00

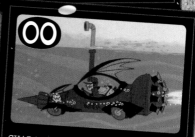

CHARACTERS: Dick Dastardly and Muttley
VEHICLE: The Mean Machine
METHOD: The World's Wackiest Racer leaves mayhem and pandemonium in his wake as he crosses the finish line first!

Recovery Plans

So, my fiendish protégé, you've been caught out in your trickery, and now you need to slip out of trouble without a backward glance. Well, it's really as simple as 'ABC'. Let me guide you in the noble art of back-sliding. Think of Villainy as a triangle of wickedness, each point feeding the other.

Lying

All you did was tell a little fibby-wibby to get yourself out of a tight spot and, of course, to protect others from the unpleasantness of Truth. Now they've caught you out and you have to think of an even bigger fib or risk losing face. The first rule: do not panic. Never be tempted to throw your hands in the air, hostage style, and cry, "Mea culpa!" before revealing your duplicity to the world. This is base stupidity. Try a brief conversational red herring to buy some time while you think of a bigger, better lie: "Oh, love the hairdo, by the way," works well. After a few more lies, the web of your deceit may have become so elaborate that you begin to believe it yourself. And when you don't realise you are lying, you really have mastered the art. Well done, you.

Cheating

Ah, my favourite pastime: cheating, or getting more for less. It's fundamental economics. Be it on the racetrack with a spot of sabotage, or in the skies with a little back-stabbing, nothing gets the old ticker pounding like a delicious dose of cheating. However, even the best ruses aren't infallible. So when the chain you've tied up your fellow contestants with breaks and they round on you before you've had a chance to get away, you need to think quickly to produce a lie that covers up your cheat (see item one). See how neatly it all fits together? It's a handy thing, this fiendishness.

Stealing

Stealing could be defined as taking something that doesn't belong to you. Or it could be defined as an intelligent act to avail yourself of something you need, quickly and without much effort. It's social Darwinism: they have it, you are more cunning than them, you utilise your natural skills to acquire said item, while depriving them of it. You win; they lose. No one likes a loser. So steal away, in the knowledge that you hold the intellectual high ground. However, if you are caught out, don't argue, simply refer to item one.

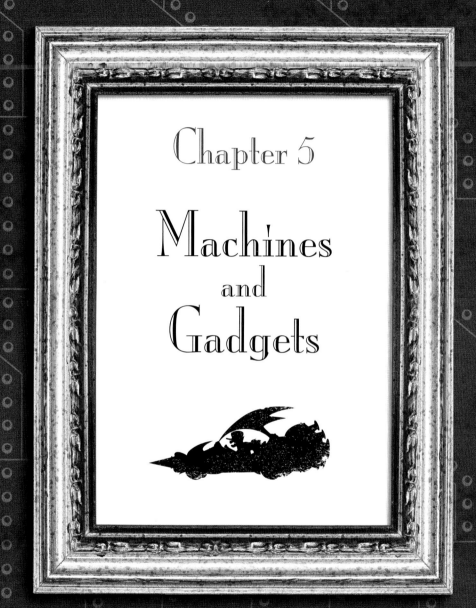

Chapter 5

Machines
and
Gadgets

TAMPERER'S TOOLKIT

> *Every craftsman needs a toolkit, and with my handy tips, you'll never be caught short without a fiendish trick up your sleeve!*

ANVIL A must for every Tamperer's Toolkit: how can you hope to catch your 'pigeon' without an ACME anvil to drop on his head? Not exactly practical to carry on your person, nevertheless this piece of kit leaves a satisfying hole in the ground when dropped from a height – even better with a pigeon pattie underneath.

CHAINS You know that sticky moment when you've nabbed 'em but you gotta keep 'em? Fill your pockets with chains and you'll never again be stuck for something to hinder your enemy's movements – even if the weight hinders yours a tad. Just beware of taking an unexpected dip when they're in your coat or you'll be sleeping with the fishes.

TACKS Ah, my personal favourite: small, discreet but highly effective. Ideal when your rivals on the racetrack are getting a bit ahead of themselves. Also effective at reserving a deckchair at the beach (note to self: next time, clean them up before taking advantage of aforementioned seat).

GLUE It's crucial that this simple substance is super-strength and fast-drying, capable of trapping and holding a charging bull or pigeon in full flight. You may need to break into a government lab to arm yourself with the appropriate compound.

GIANT RUBBER BANDS

Handy for creating super-size catapults to fling you to the front of the race or propel you towards your feathered nemesis. Beware of attacks by giant chickens looking for a meal.

OIL

Oh, the joy of the oil slick. The thrill of watching them spin and glide like a fawn on a frozen pond. Who said I've got no soul?

BOMB

This is the ultimate apparatus. Oh, the glory of that little black globe with the fizzy tail. Remember matches though, there's nothing worse than having to ask your target for a light.

MEAN MACHINE

The Mean Machine. Ah, man and machine in perfect harmony. The Mean Machine's dashboard alone provides me with a world of inspiration. I have a choice of 'weaponry', if you will, buttons for 'Low-down Tricks', 'Oil Slick', 'Fool Injection' and 'Magnetic Power'. Victory is mine! Ha-ha-harrr!

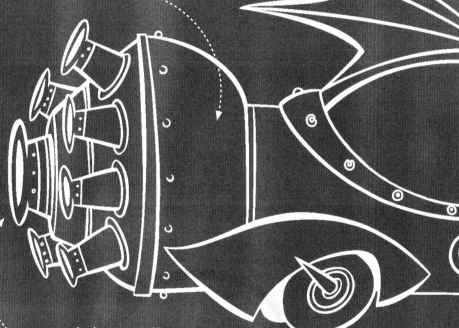

Dastardly purple bodywork for extra fiendishness.

Super turbo boosters allow incredible acceleration . . . but never seem to facilitate a win.

Foot-well holes, in case manual acceleration is required.

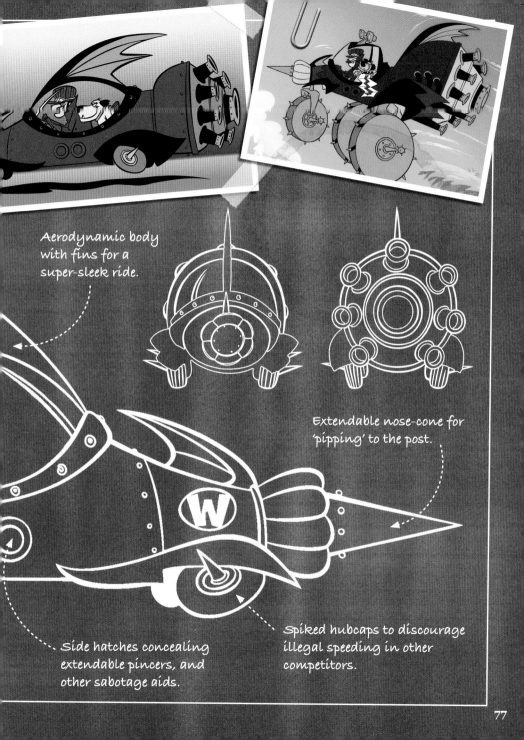

Aerodynamic body with fins for a super-sleek ride.

Extendable nose-cone for 'pipping' to the post.

Side hatches concealing extendable pincers, and other sabotage aids.

Spiked hubcaps to discourage illegal speeding in other competitors.

FLYING MACHINE

Secret compartment: if I showed you where they were, they wouldn't be secret now, would they? Suffice to say they're full of fiendish, pigeon-stopping devices, ha-hahaaar.

Sculpted bat-wing edged wings and tail: lends a fiendish feel.

Leather upholstery: oo-er, a little bit racy for some people's taste.

Me! Me, me, glorious me! What would this machine be without its flying ace? A tool is only as good as the machine that drives it, or something like that . . .

Explore your inner Red Baron: red bodywork shouts, "Stuntman of the Skies!"

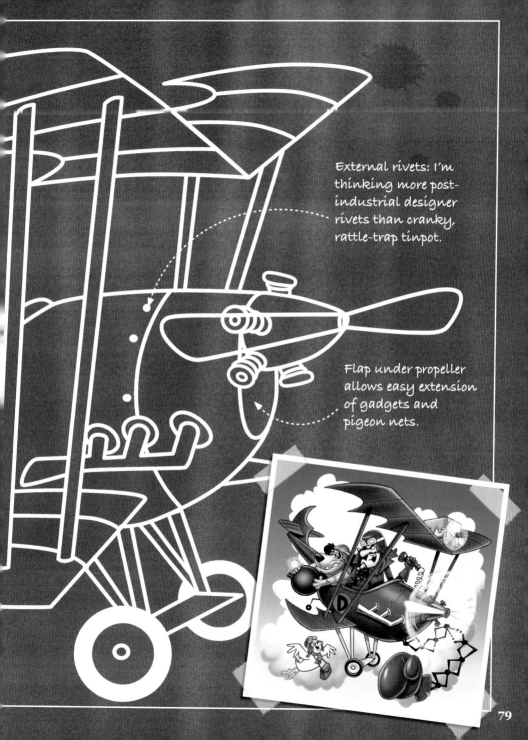

External rivets: I'm thinking more post-industrial designer rivets than cranky, rattle-trap tinpot.

Flap under propeller allows easy extension of gadgets and pigeon nets.

Chapter 6

Endgame

The Corrupt Quiz

So reader, you've learned at the knee of the Master of Mayhem, yours truly, Dick Dastardly. Try this quiz to see what kind of baddie you've become. Oh, and may I wish you the worst of luck!

Q: You drive past an attractive female driver whose vehicle's tyre, as your advanced knowledge of mechanics informs you, has a puncture. Do you:

A Stop immediately and help that damsel;

B Stop and watch, jeer patronisingly, for five minutes before offering to help;

C Whizz past, beeping your horn and laughing, leaving a cloud of dust in her face?

Q: You accidentally activate the 'Tacks Release' button on your car when you are ahead in a race. Do you:

A Stop, put your hazards on and pick them all up, every last one;

B Shrug and drive on. After all, you're in the lead and you want to keep it that way;

C Activate the 'Oil Slick' button too, just in case anyone makes it past the tacks?

Q: **Peter Perfect offers you a bribe to take a fall in a race. Do you:**

A Report him;

B Take the fall, then pocket a handsome bribe;

C Demand an advance on the bribe then blackmail him with evidence of race-fixing?

Q: **Which concepts are most important to you:**

A Family, home, love;

B Status, money, power;

C Cheating, conniving, winning?

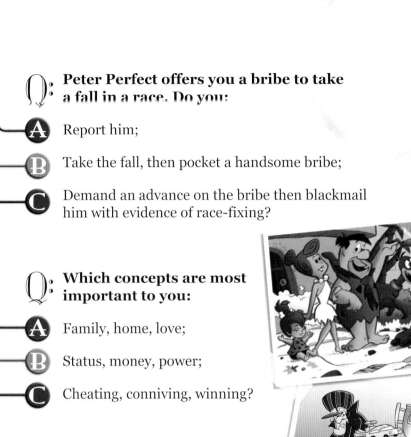

Q: **You find a poor lost puppy dog, which happens to be wearing a diamond collar, with an ID tag. Do you:**

A Call its owner straight away and offer to take it home;

B Call its owner, ask if there is a reward, then return it, having prised the gems from the collar first;

C Call its owner and demand a ransom?

Q: **Which would you choose for your headstone:**

A 'All you need is love';

B 'It's better to burn out than to fade away';

C Neither. You anticipate an unmarked grave?

Q: **You find a bag of money on the floor. Do you:**

A Donate the money to a shelter for abandoned puppies;

B Pocket some and take the rest to a police station (you can claim the rest if the owner doesn't turn up);

C Finders-keepers! Take the money and buy yourself a devilishly handsome purple coat?

A.C.M.E. PERSONALITY ANALYSER

MOSTLY AS:

FORGET IT, YOU'VE LEARNED NOTHING. JUST CLOSE THE BOOK, PUT IT DOWN AND GO POLISH YOUR HALO. YOU ARE:

PETER PERFECT »

MOSTLY BS:

NOT BAD. NOT BAD ENOUGH! COME ON, THINK: 'ME, ME, ME!' VILLAINY. CORRUPTION. GREED. ALL OF THIS COULD BE YOURS IF YOU JUST THINK BAD. YOU ARE:

OFFICER DIBBLE »

MOSTLY CS:

AHH, A VILLAIN AFTER MY OWN HEART. YOU HAVE LEARNED WELL, FRIEND. FEEL THE VELVET CLOAK OF CORRUPTION ENFOLD YOU. YOU ARE:

DICK DASTARDLY »

Your Wacky Race Car

A classic!

Every fiend needs a wacky racer, complete with devious devices and pigeon-catching gadgets. If you're too much of a chump to design and construct your own (even the boneheaded Boulder Brothers managed to build their own blundering racer!), I've provided you with a bumper sticker to cut out and slap on to your existing rust bucket – it's kudos through association, dear reader.

If you haven't got a car, try sticking the bumper sticker to your bicycle helmet. "But I haven't got a bike," I hear you whine . . . well, stop snivelling and get thinking, dunderhead! Try using your imagination for a change. Though, if you really can't think of somewhere to stick it, just leave it where it is – the page adds bulk to the book.

Yes, my fiend, cut out this dastardly piece of artwork and stick it somewhere prominent. Use tape, glue or – my favourite – tacks. Let the plebs see you are a sophisticated fiend with delectable taste in automobiles. Look, I've even drawn a dotted line to help you keep this magnificent manual neat.

MY OTHER CAR IS THE

MEAN MACHINE™

The World Is Yours!

Global domination has been a worthy goal throughout the history of mankind. Follow these steps to become Ruler of the Universe! (*Cackles wildly*.)

Steps to World Domination

• GIVE YOURSELF A FIENDISH NAME. Would 'Richard Milhous Dastardly' have achieved the same notoriety as 'Dick'? I think not.

• DRESS THE PART. That means out with the denim, and in with the dastardly flocked coat (see pages 40–41).

• IF YOU MUST, START SMALL, DEAR READER; a baddie must carefully nourish their reputation over time. For starters, swap around the price stickers in the supermarket, and then watch the chaos unfold! (I say, that is rather fiendish, isn't it?) Try raising money for your evil cause by kidnapping a rich do-gooder and demanding a ransom (and don't feel sorry for the goodie when they start to blubber: philanthropy begins with a guilty conscience).

• NOW YOUR CONFIDENCE SHOULD BE SOARING! It's time to gain control of your own country and crown yourself ruler (if this seems like too much of a leap, you could always get yourself a wacky racer and appoint yourself driver – small steps lead to Rome, or something like that.)

• WHEN YOU'RE KING OF THE ROAD, YOU MUST STAY ALERT. Squash those who oppose you! Out on the track, I keep the wannabes in line with a few carefully placed oil spills.

And finally . . .

• REVEL IN YOUR SUCCESS. Publish a dastardly guide to arch-villainy, forever knowing your name is immortalised in print . . .

K.N.

Congratulations,

friend, you've made it. On this momentous
day, I, your Master of Corruption,
Dick Dastardly, award you

....

the order of

The Knights of Naughtiness.

Rise, Sir Naughty Knighty!

Not-so-glossary

A.C.M.E the ultimate or highest point of achievement. Not sure why you'd want to get there. However, it's also a great tradename for many of the devices used in the dastardly Tamperer's Toolkit.

baddie a corrupt or evil person. The ultimate compliment. Number 2 in *The Villain's Little Book of Flattery.*

beast crit. a wild or uncontrolled animal or being. Number 6(66) in *The Villain's Little Book of Flattery.* (*Snigger.*)

blackguard a naughty person. A quaint word, but one I rather favour. Number 5 in *The Villain's Little Book of Flattery.*

corrupt jolly bad. It's music to my ears.

duplicity deceitfulness. A delightful word.

evil-doer a baddie. Rather biblical, don't you think? Number 10 in *The Villain's Little Book of Flattery.*

fiend a wicked person or devil. Number 3 in *The Villain's Little Book of Flattery.*

goon a henchman or thug.

he-y-ulp! trans. Help! (ref. Penelope Pitstop)

idiot a foolish person. Or dog.

joker a clown or fool. The Gen-er-ral often uses this term of me. Strange as I don't tell many jokes . . .

Klunk one of the dimwits that messes up every plot in *The Flying Machine.*

libertine a rather dandy baddie. Er, can't think of an example of one . . . Number 9 in *The Villain's Little Book of Flattery.*

miscreant a baddie. Number 7 in *The Villain's Little Book of Flattery.*

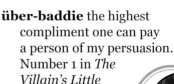

nab rhymes with grab. What I'd like to do to that pigeon!

off-screen crash an implied crash is usually accompanied by stock sound effect of crockery and glass breaking, and a cringing reaction shot.

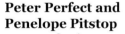

Peter Perfect and Penelope Pitstop grrr, they're so nice, it makes my skin crawl.

quibble to argue pettily – like that ridiculous mutt of mine.

Rick Rastardly that flea-bitten canine can't even pronounce my name properly.

stop that pigeon now!

tacks the perfect tool of sabotage. Who'd imagine anyone would deliberately drop a tin of tacks before a race?

über-baddie the highest compliment one can pay a person of my persuasion. Number 1 in *The Villain's Little Book of Flattery.*

villain a naughty person. Number 4 in *The Villain's Little Book of Flattery.*

Wacky Races the Ultimate, the Nirvana. Next time, I will WIN!

xylophone makes a great sound-over noise for tippy-toeing upstairs.

y me?

zebra a zebra costume makes a cunning disguise. People either think you're going to a party or are mad. They'd never suspect a bank heist. Number 8 in *The Villain's Little Book of Flattery.* Probably.